CHESS
80 CLASSIC PROBLEMS

THIS IS A CARLTON BOOK

Published in Great Britain in 2009 by
Carlton Books Limited
20 Mortimer Street
London W1T 3JW

A CIP catalogue for this book is available from the
British Library.

ISBN 978-1-84732-347-7

Printed in China

CHESS

80 CLASSIC PROBLEMS

—— Leonard Barden & Erwin Brecher ——

One Move and You're Dead!

To Mary, in honour of the reunion we never managed

Contents

About Erwin Brecher

Erwin Brecher was educated in Vienna, Czechoslovakia and London. He studied physics, economics and engineering to become AMIMechE and AMIProdE.

He majored in psychology for his PhD. He joined the Czech army in 1937, and at the outbreak of war escaped to London via Switzerland. He worked for De Havilland on aircraft design, and in 1946 formed a group of companies active in international trade and finance. In 1963 his companies were acquired by a listed investment trust. He was appointed to the main board and to the board of its banking subsidiary.

In 1972 Erwin Brecher became CEO of an international financial group with offices in New York, Rio de Janeiro, Switzerland, Athens and Istanbul. He specialised in developing a technique known as International Counter-trade in connection with which he travelled extensively.

In 1974 he became a Name at Lloyds of London. In 1978 he acquired control of a quoted investment trust and served as its chairman until his retirement in 1984. Erwin Brecher is a shareholder and on the board of MBA International, a specialist recruitment company. He is also CEO of a company of financial consultants (established in 1947). In addition he continues to act as adviser to private and listed companies.

He is the author of twenty-two books on non-fiction subjects, published in six languages by US and European companies. In September 1995 he was awarded the Order of Merit in Gold by the city of Vienna in recognition of his literary achievements.

Erwin Brecher, a member of Mensa, has been a regular contributor to magazines and radio in the UK and abroad.

About Leonard Barden

Leonard Barden was born in Croydon and studied history at Whitgift School and Balliol College, Oxford. After leaving university he made chess writing his profession, combining it with international play. He was British co-champion in 1954, represented England in four chess Olympiads, and was Bobby Fischer's partner in the only consultation game Fischer ever played—on BBC radio. He was chess adviser to Jim Slater in 1972 when the financier saved the Fischer vs. Boris Spassky world title match in Reykjavik by doubling the prize fund.

In the 1970s Barden was a presenter on the BBC2 televised *Master Game* series, advised Lloyds Bank on its chess sponsorship which ran for nearly 20 years, and administered the national Grand Prix. He managed the England junior squad in the 1970s and 1980s when the country produced a record number of grandmasters, and was the first to predict in print that Garry Kasparov (then 11) would become world champion and that Nigel Short (then 9) would become Kasparov's challenger.

Barden has written chess columns for the *Guardian* (weekly) and *London Evening Standard* (daily) for more than half a century, and also contributes weekly to the *Financial Times*. In February 2008, he broke the record for the longest running chess column by a single writer.

Introduction

A proven way to enhance your chess results is through studying tactics. The buzz word, the cool skill to acquire is pattern recognition, an ability which all the world's leading grandmasters have developed to a high level. Pattern recognition enables you to spot that the position in front of you has key similarities to the one you saw in another game or in our puzzle book.

This quick eye for opportunities is definitely a method which can be learnt. Just ten or fifteen minutes a day sharpening your combinative vision will soon start to pay off in your better alertness for practical chances when they occur in your own over-the-board or internet games.

In *Chess: 80 Classic Problems* we have chosen the most dynamic and destructive tactical patterns, positions where the winning move forces instant checkmate, resignation or decisive advantage. Quite often such climaxes are the result of sustained and prolonged attacking pressure, and the final move may be make or break, where the winner has already burnt boats by sacrificing material.

Tactical opportunities can occur in any phase of the game, from the opening moves to the ending. However, you can and should maximise your chances of reaching tactically rich positions right from the opening moves. Make good use of gambits, pawn sacrifices aiming at the fast piece development which is the necessary prelude to a decisive assault on your opponent's king. Gambits are rare in high-class international tournaments and matches where the grandmasters are experts in defence, but it is entirely different in social, club and internet games. There attack and initiative is at a premium, and in practical play you can normally expect defensive errors from your opponent.

Gambits we recommend include the Goring 1 e4 e5 2 Nf3 Nc6 3 d4 exd4 4 c3 dxc3 5 Bc4, the Morra 1 e4 c5 2 d4 cxd4 c3 or the Wing 1 e4 c5 2 b4 against the Sicilian Defence, the Fantasy 1 e4 c6 2 d4 d5 3 f3 against the Caro-Kann, and the Whitaker 1 e4 e6 2 d4 d5 3 Be3 dxe4 4 f3 against the French. You prefer 1 d4 openings? Then try out the Blackmar 1 d4 d5 2 Nc3 Nf6 3 e4 dxe4 4 f3. Another all-purpose attacking system against the fianchettoed bishops (Bg7) which are common in defences like the Sicilian, King's Indian and Pirc is to develop Be3, f3, Qd2, 0-0-0 and h4-h5 to open up the h file.

When it comes to the middle game and the real tactics, a common theme of many of our puzzles is that the attacker uses several pieces to storm the king's defences. And the chances of success are greater if the target king is tucked away in the corner of the board. When that happens, the tactics can be launched with a queen and rook sometimes supported by knight or bishop. Puzzles 5, 7, 8, 9, 15, 18, 22, 27, 41, 46, 48, 53, 59, 62, 66 and 67 are all good examples of plans and formations which often recur.

If your opponent brings out his army too slowly and you can open up the centre before his king is castled, that provides another scenario for a tactician. Look at puzzles 4, 13, 23, 35, 39 and 78. The winning ideas may look complex, but simply keep in mind the basic idea that a king which is still at or near its original e8 square with an open centre is a natural target.

A third format which catches many kings is the rear rank. His castled Majesty feels snug behind a trio of unmoved or scarcely moved pawn guards until the attackers burst through the back door. Look at puzzles 14, 49, 55, 57 and 77 for examples of how a rear rank tactic works. In amateur chess it can occur more easily, as a single rook swoops down to the back row.

Kings are not the only target for tacticians. Forks and skewers, where a small value piece simultaneously attacks two larger ones and gains material, form the bread of tactical chess where attacks on the king are the cake. For a quick course on forks and skewers, try to solve puzzles 1, 15, 25, 65 (a position on which one of your authors dismally failed) and 73.

It is a mistake to believe that tactics stop when you reach the endgame. They are just different. The ultimate target in many endgames is to queen a pawn, and to achieve that may require finesse and trickery. Puzzles 11, 12, 68 and 70 are all good illustrations of how and where a sacrifice will allow a pawn to reach the eighth rank.

Studying grandmaster chess and identifying the winning thought wave can be really enjoyable and even uplifting. A memorable work of fiction provides this graphic insight:

Stefan Zweig, the Austrian writer, who committed suicide in 1942, in emigration, contributed a whimsical story to chess literature in his book Schachnovelle. It is about a Viennese lawyer, identified only as Dr B. He was an ardent anti-Nazi and when Hitler's army occupied Austria in April 1938 one of his clerks betrayed him to the Gestapo.

As he was suspected of being connected with resistance groups, he was singled out for special treatment. Instead of sending him to a concentration camp, the Gestapo incarcerated him in a tiny windowless cell in the basement of their headquarters, the Hotel Metropole in Vienna.

While his barest physical needs were taken care of, he was not allowed any human contact nor was anything provided – books, newspapers, pencil or paper – to occupy his mind.

Before long his complete isolation and lack of any external stimuli began to affect his sanity. When the Nazi jailers assumed that their tactics had succeeded in breaking his spirit, he was taken for questioning to an SS major who, to wear him down further, kept him waiting for two hours in a small windowless office.

Dr B., pacing nervously up and down, suddenly noticed a little well-worn book, discarded in a waste paper basket. A book! It was like water to a man in the desert, dying of thirst.

During the interrogation he was incoherent and hardly conscious. Back in his cell he opened the book with trembling hands, only to be devastated when he saw that the book that was to be a treasure, saving him from going mad, was a collection of 150 chess games played by grandmasters.

After recovering from the initial shock, he started to study the moves again and again until eventually he knew the many variations, from opening gambit to endgame, by heart. By the time the German army surrendered and Dr B. was released, he had become an expert player.

As a final twist, Zweig tells the story of a cruise during which Dr B., an unknown in the chess world, defeats a grandmaster.

Some of the positions in this book have previously appeared in Leonard Barden's chess columns in the *Evening Standard*, *Guardian*, *Financial Times*, and Australian and New Zealand papers. They are published here with updated texts.

Now let's get on with the puzzles. The tactics are there, waiting for you to find them.

ERWIN BRECHER AND LEONARD BARDEN

The Puzzles

Sir George Thomas vs. Alfred Brinckmann

Budapest 1929.

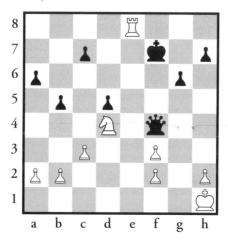

This is one of the historical games where we would have liked to have been present, just to observe the frisson between the opponents. Thomas was a natural, aristocratic gentleman, very conscious of correct behaviour and protocol, conservative in his views, and a player who had shone at badminton and tennis before transferring to international chess. Brinckmann was the first openly gay chess master, who caused a scandal at Rogaska-Slatina the same year as Budapest when he propositioned Salo Flohr, then an innocent 20-year-old and later a world-title challenger. Often when such irregular occurrences took place in European tournaments, the organisers came to Thomas and asked how the problem would be dealt with in England. The London baronet's usual stiff reply was: "It would never happen in England."

How did he score the point as White (to play)?

Aleksei Alexandrov vs. Alexey Lusto
Elista 1998.

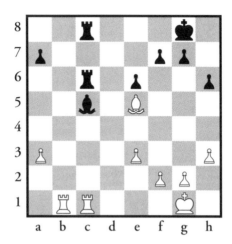

Two similar first name spellings, and two virtually identical armies. With king, two rooks, bishop and five pawns on each side, the prognosis seems to be for a mass exchange of rooks on the open c file followed by a quick handshake. In fact, the higher ranked Alexandrov had seen deeper into the position. His next turn as White (to play) proved so strong that Lusto soon has to concede material and resign. What was White's winning move?

David Bronstein vs. Grigory Levenfish

USSR championship 1946.

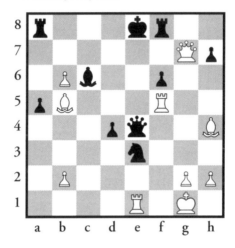

Bronstein (White, to play) was the rising star of Soviet chess, who later tied a controversial world-title match with Mikhail Botvinnik. And it was Botvinnik, the dedicated Communist Party member, who was Levenfish's bête noire. He had won the 1937 USSR title but was obliged to defend it against the higher-ranked Botvinnik, whom state sport bosses were grooming for the world championship. Unexpectedly, Levenfish tied the series so kept his crown, but party bureaucrats denied him international opportunities, which went instead to Botvinnik and his trainer.

Finally, in 1947, Levenfish travelled as a reserve to London with the Soviet team, which took on Britain in its first ever match in the West.

Arriving at Holborn Town Hall, where hundreds of spectators queued, he was greeted by Paul List, an old Lithuanian friend whom he had last met in 1911. They chatted for a few minutes... as a hidden KGB agent watched and took notes. Levenfish was never again allowed outside eastern Europe.

What was Bronstein's winning move in the diagram?

Reuben Fine vs. Herman Steiner

Hollywood 1945.

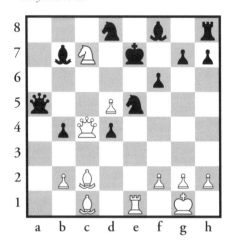

It was a unique occasion in tournament chess, where the grandmasters played in front of a fascinated audience of movie stars. Steiner, the US title runner-up, was the chief organiser and promoter of the event, and used his contacts to set up photo-shoots to publicise the contest. In one the actresses Linda Darnell and Mitzi Mayfair posed scantily clothed, playing a game watched by a bemused Reuben Fine, then a psychologist and world championship contender. But Fine was at his sharpest in the position illustrated, where the white army has trapped Steiner's king in mid board.

Can you spot White's winning move?

Mark Taimanov vs. Alexander Tolush
USSR championship 1954.

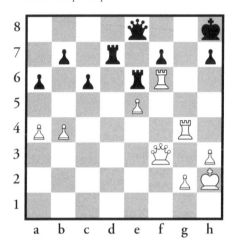

There is an affinity, though sometimes conflicting, between chess and music, which Taimanov embodied. He was ranked among the world top ten grandmasters for the best part of a decade while simultaneously touring the USSR giving piano duets with his first wife Lyubov Bruk.

Positions like this, where White's queen and rooks are in harmonious control of the board, suited Taimanov's style but were just the opposite for his hard-drinking opponent who liked dashing and offbeat attacks. Here material is level and White's e5 pawn is twice menaced so the game looks drawish, but Taimanov's next white move proved so strong that Tolush conceded defeat.

Can you spot White's winner?

Olaf Barda vs. Jan Foltys

Marianske Lazne 1951.

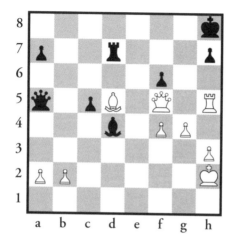

This puzzle illustrates the maxim that bishops of opposite colours (White's B operates on light squares, Black's on dark), which increase the chances of an endgame draw, can help an attacker in the middle game.

Norwegian Barda's d5 bishop supports his queen and rook in targeting the black king, while Czech Foltys's d4 bishop sets up the plan of Qd2+ Kg3? Qf2 mate. Black's formation also has a subtler concept. The obvious choice for White (to move) is 1 Qxd7 but then comes Qd2+ 2 Bg2 (2 Kg3 Qf2 mate) Bg1+! 3 Kxg1 Qxd7 and Black is ahead. The Scandinavian champion therefore needs a drastic solution, and Barda's answer to the puzzle earned a brilliancy prize.

What was White's winning move?

David Bronstein vs. Alexander Kotov

Moscow championship 1946.

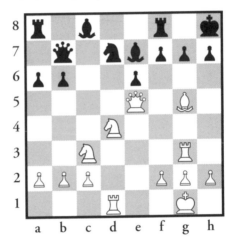

This was a significant moment for Bronstein, the then 22-year-old Ukrainian who became a world title challenger despite his father being condemned to a labour camp. His dynamic repertoire with the white pieces included the dashing King's Gambit 1 e4 e5 2 f4 and he also scored with impressive attacks against the Sicilian 1 e4 c5. So the wily and experienced Kotov preferred the Caro-Kann 1 e4 c6 and tried to lure Bronstein into a premature attack. His last turn Nf6-d7 menaced White's e5 queen and also planned the sequence 1 Qe3 f6 2 Bf4 e5 3 Nf5 (with the idea exf4 4 Qxe7) Bc5! when Black gains material. Bronstein's next move came as complete shock to his opponent, decided the game immediately, impressed experts worldwide, and helped secure the winner's reputation as one of the most creative attackers.

What happened?

Ulf Andersson vs. Kenneth Rogoff
Olot 1971.

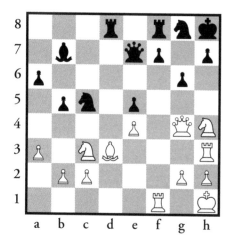

Quite a few professional chess masters who abandon the game due to uncertain income successfully transform themselves into computer programmers or financial traders. Rogoff did much better than that. The one-time grandmaster became an economics professor at Harvard, then a director of the International Monetary Fund.

Here Rogoff was up against one of the best grandmasters in the world at the time. He hasn't made any blunders, but Sweden's Andersson has lined up queen, two rooks and a knight against the troubled black king.

What was White's winning move?

Etienne Bacrot vs. Lother Vogt
Arusa 1996.

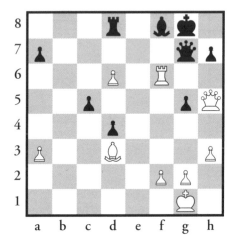

This puzzle looks headed for a draw. Current French number one Bacrot, then a teenage prodigy, has an attack, but Germany's Vogt threatens both Qxf6 and Rxd6. Expert spectators began to analyse 1 Bc4+ Kh8 2 Rf7 Qg6 3 Qxg6 hxg6 4 Rxa7 Rxd6, when White is a pawn ahead but Black's united central pair create serious drawing chances. Bishops of opposite colours (Bacrot's bishop operates on light squares, Vogt's on dark) often favour an attacker, and Bacrot had spotted earlier that the c5-d4 duo could restrict Vogt's own pieces. The finish was a surprise.

What was White's winning move?

Southsea 1950.

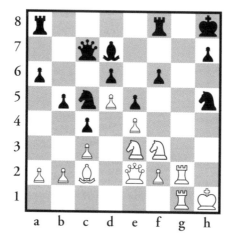

Penrose, then 16, was England's brightest prospect. He had impressively defeated the world-ranked veterans Ewfim Bogolyubov and Savielly Tartakover earlier in the tournament, and seemed en route to first prize. Bisguier was America's best young player, the leader of a generation that later included Bobby Fischer. He was serving with the US Army, and persuaded his commanding officer to give him special leave to compete at Southsea.

The game looked good for Penrose as his knights infiltrated round the flanks of Bisguier's compact force, and in the diagram Black has the powerful threat of Nf4 forking White's queen and rook. But Bisguier (White, to play) had seen further. His next turn won the game, and at the end of the tournament the American shared first prize half a point ahead of Penrose.

What happened?

Dibyendu Barua vs. Viktor Korchnoi

Lloyds Bank London 1982.

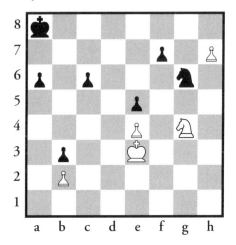

India is currently a leading chess nation thanks to the exploits of World Champion Vishy Anand who is his country's most popular sportsman next to the cricketer Sachin Tendulkar. But the game that first convinced the Indian media and sponsors that chess could make a major impact occurred earlier, when Anand was still an unknown schoolboy. Korchnoi was nicknamed "the Leningrad lip" for his outspoken defection from the Soviet Union, and had just played two world title matches against the USSR's Anatoly Karpovs.

He was top seed at Lloyds Bank and expected to crush his teenage opponent. But Barua conceived a profound strategy, taking on an endgame two pawns down which looked lost, but where Korchnoi's king was out of play. Now three impressive and visual moves forced the great man's resignation. A thoughtful UK journalist phoned the *Chess Mate* magazine editor in Chennai/ Madras in the middle of the night local time to tell him the big news. Sleepy Manuel Aaron recorded the final few moves and relayed them to TV and newspaper sources. Barua's finish made the front page, and chess became a major sport in India. What was White's winning trick?

Ulf Andersson vs. Bengt Horberg

Swedish championship 1969.

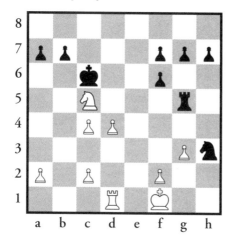

Andersson was then the rising star of Western Europe, tipped to rival Russia's Anatoly Karpov as a contender for the world title. The Swede had wonderfully subtle strategic skills, but as his career developed he acquired an eccentric taste for marathon endgames with tiny advantages. The result was that he drew far too many games to succeed at top level. The position illustrated looks a typical Andersson grind, but surprisingly it took him just one move to force resignation.

What was Andersson's winning move?

London 1851.

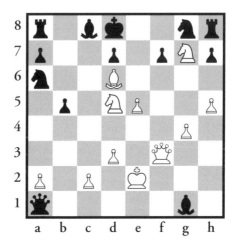

It was only an off-hand friendly game at Simpson's-in-the-Strand and not part of the 1851 tournament which Anderssen also won, but the finish acquired the title of "The Immortal Game" and remains among the best known in chess history. It also put Simpson's on the map as a centre of chess excellence.

In the diagram, Anderssen (White, to move) has already sacrificed both rooks, one to Black's queen and the other to the g1 bishop. But most of Kieseritzky's army remains unmoved from the start position, while White's queen, knights and bishop are all on menacing squares. White must act fast before Black's queen becomes active by Qc1.

How did Anderssen join the immortals?

Dr James Aitken vs. Roland Payne

British championship, Whitby 1962.

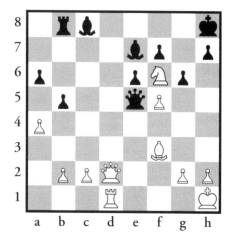

Material is level, but White's knight appears in a tangle. The obvious 1 Ng4 allows Qxf5 or Qxb2, while the fork 1 Nd7 Bxd7 2 Qxd7 is countered by Rd8! 3 Qxe7 Rxd1+ 4 Bxd1 Qe1 mate. Black's hopes were shattered by White's next turn, which forced immediate resignation.

The winner was several times Scottish champion, wrote a scholarly PhD thesis on the Spanish Inquisition, and cracked German codes at Bletchley Park during the Second World War. The loser, then a young talent, became one of London's best bridge and chess amateurs.

What was White's winning move?

Bob Wade vs. Graham Boxall

Bognor 1963.

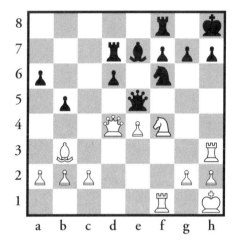

Twice British champion Wade was the UK's leading veteran player. Until his death in 2008 at the ago of 87, he still took part regularly in tournaments and matches, and was one of the best instructional talkers in the game.

In this position Black's defence looks solid, and he has just offered to exchange queens, but Wade had prepared a tactical coup which forced his opponent to resign.

What happened?

Peter Leko vs. Lazaro Bruzon

Corus Wijk aan Zee 2005.

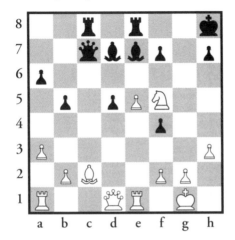

Hungary's Leko needed a win as White (to move) to secure first prize. White's c2 bishop is manaced, and the obvious play 1 Rc1 Bxf5 2 Bxf5 Qxc1 3 Qxc1 Rxc1 4 Rxc1 Bf8 (threat Rxe5) leads to a probably drawn endgame. But Leko had seen far ahead to this position.

What was White's next turn which forced Black's resignation?

Liviu-Dieter Nisipeanu vs. Vadim Milov

European championship, Warsaw 2005.

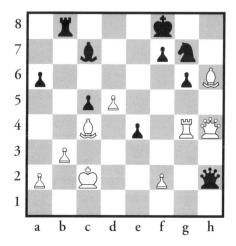

Nisipeanu reached the Fide world semi-finals at Las Vegas 1999, and was then scorned by Garry Kasparov as "just a tourist". The jibe was widely reported, but Romania's number one responded with his games and has forged ahead with a series of impressive results in tactical style. In 2005 he became European champion, outscoring a flock of higher-rated opponents.

Here as White (to move) he has level material, while Switzerland's Milov has just offered the exchange of queens. 1 Qxh2 Bxh2 2 Rxe4 wins a pawn, but White would still face a long endgame. Nisipeanu's choice was stronger, so much so that Milov immediately resigned. There was still a twist, for many amateurs who saw the final position didn't understand Black's surrender and thought he had resigned in a superior position.

Can you find the winning play and what the spectators missed?

Luke McShane vs. Branko Damljanovic

England vs. Serbia, European team championship, Gothenburg 2005.

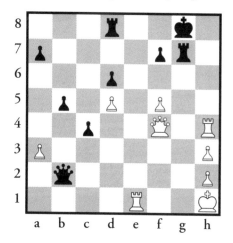

London's top grandmaster, McShane, 25, led the national team in style, scoring six out of nine by imaginative attacking play. McShane's secret was his unorthodox white opening repertoire with 1 d4 d5 2 Bf4 and 1 d4 Nf6 2 Bg5 which netted three of his wins, including this diagram. Material is level and at first glance the position looks good for Black, who threatens Qg2 mate, has a solidly guarded king, and is ready to use his queen to support the c4 pawn's advance. McShane had seen further, and his next turn forced the Serbian grandmaster's speedy resignation.

What happened?

Stewart Haslinger vs. Michael Waters

Smith & Williamson British Championship, Douglas 2005.

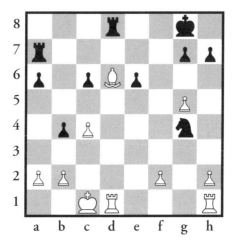

Haslinger, then 23, finished joint second in the national-title contest and showed he is the best young master in the North. This position looks harmless, level material without obvious advantage, but it provides a good example of what can occur in the frequent chessboard battles between a bishop and a knight. Many novices fear the knight's power to fork two stronger pieces in a double attack, which could occur here if Black went Nxf2 menacing both white rooks. But Haslinger knew that knights are best in blocked positions, and at their worst on an open board against a free-ranging bishop. He took clever advantage, and just one move sufficed to force his opponent's resignation.

What was White's winner, and why did Black give up?

Levon Aronian vs. Bragim Khamrakulov

Bratislava 1993.

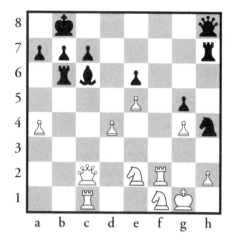

Most of today's elite grandmasters have come up through the ranks of junior competitions. And junior in chess can be very young indeed. There's an official world championship for under-tens, while London stages an annual city title contest for under-eights with merit awards for those aged five or six. Armenia's Aronian was only ten when he won the position illustrated in the world under-twelves. Now, aged 27, he ranks eleventh in the world.

The position seems unclear and confused. White controls the centre, Black tries to sneak round the edge. But it took just one turn for Aronian to force resignation.

What happened?

Emanuel Berg vs. Evgeny Bareev

European team championship, Gothenburg 2005.

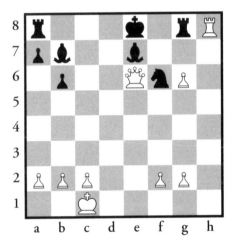

The mighty Russians were humbled, finishing fourteenth for their worst-ever result in international competition. They fielded a weakened team, but were still top seeds. One factor was that several times opponents came up with opening novelties, a speciality of the old Soviet grandmasters.

This position was the end of the most brilliant game against a Russian, where the little-known Swede sacrificed several pieces to devastate Bareev's king. At first glance Black is still in the game with rook, two bishops and a knight for White's extra queen. The obvious play is 1 Rxg8+ Nxg8 2 Qxg8+ but Black holds on by Kd7 3 Qh7 Bd5. After Berg's actual choice, Bareev had to resign.

What was White's winner, and why did Black give up?

Andras Adorjan vs. Anatoly Karpov

Hoogeveen 2003.

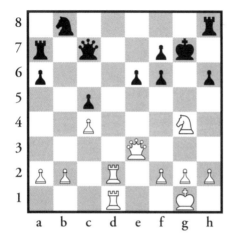

Hungary's grandmaster Adorjan is an unconventional bohemian who likes to dress in strikingly coloured shirts and runs a permanent crusade on behalf of the black pieces. His classic book *Black is OK!* demonstrated a variety of methods by which the second player can seize an early initiative. But Adorjan, who once qualified as a world-title candidate, can also handle the white side with dexterity, and in the position shown he has outplayed the chess legend and former world champion Karpovs. White's rooks control the open d file, and his queen and knight are actively placed, while in contrast the black army is reduced to passive defence on the back rows to try and protect the Russian king. One more move sufficed to show Karpov that his position was hopeless.

How did the game end?

Miguel Najdorf vs. Amateur

Buenos Aires 1942.

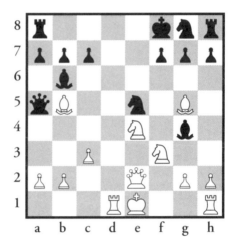

At the start of September 1939, the world chess Olympiad was in full swing in Buenos Aires, and Poland had a narrow edge over Germany in the race for the gold medals. Then, just as the Polish players were ready to start the next round, the country's ambassador to Argentina arrived at the playing hall to inform them that German Stuka bombers were attacking Warsaw. Dumb move! The demoralised Poles lost a key match, Germany won the Olympiad by half a point ahead of Poland, and Najdorf and other Jews on the team remained in South America for the duration. Desperate for contact with his family, Najdorf gave a series of high-profile, blindfold exhibitions in the hope that reports of them would reach Europe. Later he tragically discovered that his entire family had perished in concentration camps. This was his most impressive blindfold finish.

How did White (to move) force victory?

Max Dlugy vs. Stephen Stoyko

Cherry Hill 1991.

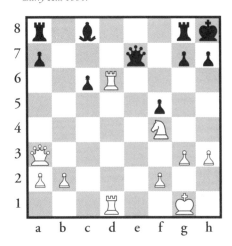

Former junior world champion Dlugy became the youngest US Chess Federation president. Here as White (to move) against a lower ranked opponent, he has established a risk-free advantage conceding Black no counterplay. Masters just love positions like this where the opponent has no activity. White's queen, rooks and knight all cover key squares, while Black's army is confined to the two rear rows. There is still work to do, since the obvious play 1 Rxc6 Qxa3 2 bxa3 Bb7 brings Black's bishop to life, while White's extra doubled pawn means little. Another plausible attempt 1 Qd3, tripling queen and rooks on the d file, is met by c5 with the idea of Bb7 Rd7 Qe4. Dlugy found a much better idea, effectively knocking out Black with a single punch.

What happened?

Harry Golombek vs. Nicholas Rossolimo

Venice 1950.

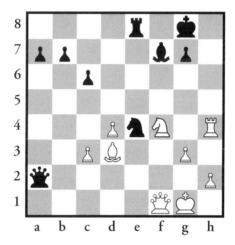

Golombek in his heyday was the best-known personality in UK chess. He was a wartime Enigma code-breaker, a three-time British champion and *Times* correspondent, and wrote a best-selling Penguin for novices. He was at his playing peak around 1950, and later became referee at several world-title matches.

Here material is level and although White has an attack, Black can hope for a counterpunch like 1 Qh3? Qf2+ 2 Kh1 Nxg3+! 3 gxh3 Re1+ and wins. Golombek found a clever tactic against an opponent who was then number one for France.

What was White's winning move?

Rogelio Antonio vs. Dao Thein Hai

Malaysian Open 2005.

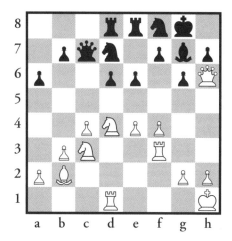

With China and India aiming to become chess superpowers and smaller Far East nations benefiting from the increased tournament activity, Asia is currently the growth area for chess. The game was given official status in last year's Asian Games in Qatar. Althought Beijing did not feature chess as a sport at the 2008 Olympic Games, Qatar plans to bid for the 2016 Olympics and has said that chess will be part of the package.

In the position illustrated, White is attacking, and though Black seems to have a solid defensive formation it took the Philippines master Antonio (White, to play) just one turn to induce his Vietnamese opponent to resign.

What happened?

Bragi Thorfinsson vs. Amar Gunnarson

Reykjavik 2006.

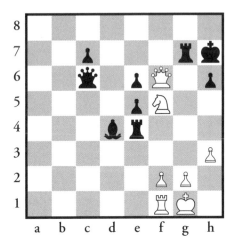

It was a full two hours straight TV chess, a remarkable sight anywhere –
but maybe not in Iceland, which has the highest number of grandmasters
relative to population of any major country.

The two experts were in the final stages of their speed game when
Thorfinsson, with a lost position, sacrificed a rook for a crude trap. He
hoped that Black would fall for exf5?? Qxc6. Gunnarson planned Qd7, but
the clock made him panic and he went Kg8?? allowing Qxg7 mate. Then
came the most unexpected twist. The TV station got a call from a viewer
pointing out a spectacular black win in the diagram. It was Bobby Fischer,
now a Icelandic citizen, watching the programme, and giving a rare
indication that he still follows real chess.

Of course, Bobby was right. What should Black play?

Hugh Alexander vs. Vincenzo Castaldi

Hilversum 1947.

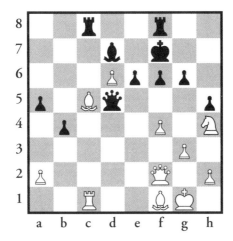

Alexander, the best British player of his time, was a true amateur who competed in his time off from code-breaking German and Russian ciphers. In World War Two he was one of the top Enigma code experts at Bletchley Park. The Foreign Office would not allow him to lead the England team at the Moscow 1956 Olympiad nor even in 1952 at Helsinki, which the mandarins thought too near the Soviet border. Alexander specialised in giant-killing, beat two world champions, and played in an imaginative, unorthodox style. His primer *Learn Chess*, written nearly half a century ago, is still one of the best books for novices.

This puzzle is from a world title eliminator where Alexander (White, to move) has bishop and knight against rook and pawn, which looks about equal. Some would prefer Black's threat of Bc6 and Qh1 mate, but Alexander saw deeper.

Can you find White's winning move?

Pentala Harikrishna vs. Giovanni Vescovi

World Cup, Khanty Mansiysk 2005.

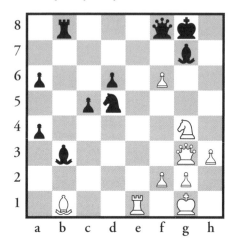

The Siberian city of Khanty Mansiysk has winter temperatures of −15°C, so both the teenager from Chennai/Madras and the Brazilian from Rio were at a disadvantage. Vescovi won their first game, so the Indian number three needed to win this position as White (to move). He staked all on his king's side attack, sacrificing a bishop while Vescovi hoped to promote his a4 pawn. Now the obvious 1 fg7 Qxg7 leaves the outcome unclear. Hari found a better choice which proved so strong that it forced Black's immediate resignation.

What was White's winning move?

Levon Aronian vs. Francisco Vallejo Pons

World Cup 2005.

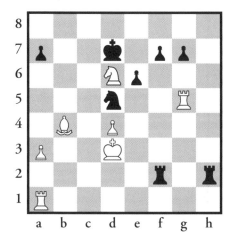

Aronian won the $1.5 million event but said afterwards that he was dissatisfied with his performance. A strange comment from a grandmaster achieving his lifetime-best result, but the diagram explained it. Only by good fortune and the help of his opponent did the 23-year-old avoid a disaster that could have knocked him out of the tournament in the last 16. Although Vallejo Pons (Black, to move) is bishop for two pawns down, his doubled rooks on the seventh menace the white king. Whether through time shortage or a total misjudgement, the Spaniard continued with the bizarrely passive 1...a6? Instead Black has an immediate win, and there are two ways to do it.

Can you do better than the grandmaster?

Gata Kamsky vs. Levon Aronian

Corus Wijk aan Zee 2006.

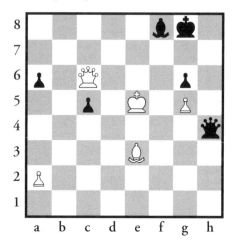

Strong grandmasters flinch when confronted with an endgame like this puzzle. World Cup winner Aronian (Black, to move) is a pawn up against American's top-ranked grandmaster, so on principle the Armenian should seek to play for a win. But how? White's queen menaces both the a6 and g6 pawns, which the black queen on the edge is poorly placed to defend. Most experts would settle for 1...Qh2+ 2 Bf4 Qe2+ (if Qxa2 3 Qxg6+) 3 Qe4 Qxe4+ forcing off the queens, but a win would then still be difficult because 4 Kxe4 Kf7 5 Kd5 keeps the black king boxed in. There is a hidden answer, and Aronian found it. He made just one move, Kamsky stared at the board for several minutes in disbelief at its strength, then the New Yorker resigned.

Can you find Black's subtle winner?

Yrjo Verho vs. Ali Krogius

Helsinki 1932.

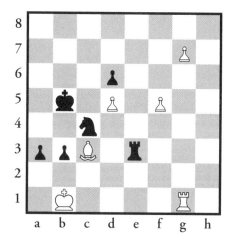

The players were unknowns – and the black player was no relation to the Soviet grandmaster Nikolai Krogius, who gave Boris Spassky and Anatoly Karpov some banal psychological advice for their world-title matches. Here the Finnish Krogius looks up against it. White's g7 pawn is just one square off queening, and if Black gives up a rook for it by Re8 g8Q Rxg8 Rxg8 then Black's own pawn duo are easily stopped. Black (to play) found a brilliant answer and a rare type of checkmate.

Can you spot Black's winner and why White had to surrender?

Loek van Wely vs. Lucas Brunner
Biel 1997.

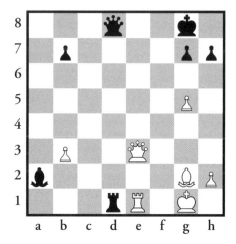

They call the Dutch grandmaster "King Loek", a reference not only to his fine play but to his height of over two metres. Dutch grandmasters have often been tall. When their team led by ex-world champion Max Euwe visited London for an England vs. Holland match, the impression was of a squad of high jumpers. Both Euwe and his successor Jan Timman reached the international super-elite, so van Wely naturally has the same ambition, but so far the top 30-40 grandmasters has been his limit.

Here material is level with queens, rooks and bishops on an open board. It took just one turn for King Loek to force resignation.

What happened?

Andre Lilienthal vs. Ivan Aramanovic

Moscow 1945.

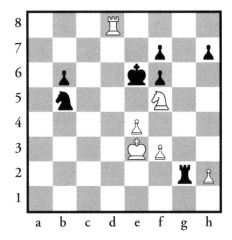

Lilienthal, 97, is the oldest living grandmaster and knew all the world champions from Emanuel Lasker to Garry Kasparovs. He was a survivor, a Hungarian born in Moscow who avoided trouble during several decades in the old Soviet Union and now lives in Budapest. Lilienthal was never the greatest strategist, but his tactical eye gave him some memorable victories over eminent players.

Here as White (to move) he is a pawn down in a simple endgame where his opponent threatens Rxh2, increasing the advantage. However, it took just one turn for Lilienthal to demonstrate victory.

What was White's winning move?

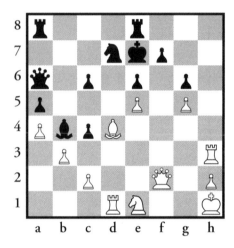

Both players were contemporaries of Garry Kasparov, and years later
the all-time number one was looking for aides in his world title campaign
against Anatoly Karpovs. He remembered Vladimirov's studious approach
and enlisted him as a trainer cum researcher, but the job ended in tears.
Vladimirov was publicly shamed and dismissed when Kasparov declared
that his coach had been selling opening secrets to the Karpov camp.
Vladimirov denied everything and still does, but the damage was done.
Though he has since been Asian champion and trainer to the Indian
national team, it's the Kasparov episode that people remember.

How did Vladimirov win as White (to move)?

Andrei Volokitin vs. Vladimir Chukhil

Alusha 1998.

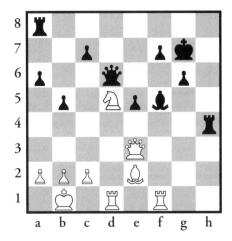

Novices are taught that three pawns are roughly equal to a bishop or knight, but that's only true as you approach the endgame or if the pawns are well advanced with good support. More typical are positions like this puzzle where White's d5 knight is worth significantly more than Black's static king's side pawns giving only flimsy protection to their monarch which the white army is eyeing up for attack. Volokitin, 22, is among a group of talented young Ukrainian grandmasters who won the 2004 world team Olympiad, and he took just one turn to force Black's resignation.

What happened?

Alexey Shirov vs. Alex Areschenko

Aerosvit Yalta 2006.

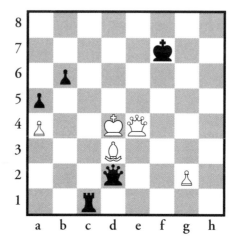

Former world finalist Shirov likes to live dangerously on the chessboard. The Latvian-born grandmaster who now represents Spain is always ready to consider sacrificing pieces and pawns for nebulous compensation or, as here, to boldly use his king as an attacking weapon. His Ukrainian opponent was too respectful. Rather than allow the diagram, Areschenko swapped off the queens a few moves earlier and settled for half a point when he was on the brink of victory.

What should Black play?

John Nunn vs. Jan Smeets

Experience vs. Youth, Amsterdam 2006.

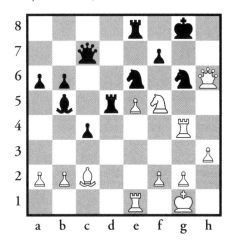

Former Olympiad gold medallist Nunn retired from tournament play in 2005 on his fiftieth birthday. He is one of the game's best writers, and his Gambit company has published several excellent instruction books. Nunn made a rare comeback for the veteran grandmasters against a team of rising talent, and although his overall total was only 3.5 out of 10, his win in this puzzle was the best finish of the event.

White has already sacrificed a knight to besiege the black king, and his next turn proved so decisive that Black immediately conceded defeat.

What was White's winning move?

Teimour Radjabov vs. Vishy Anand

World Blitz Championship, Israel 2006.

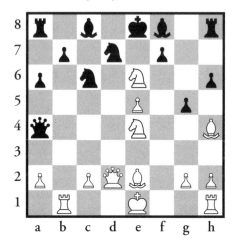

Blitz, where the entire game encompasses ten minutes, has become the new chess spectator sport. A web camera shows the grandmasters making their moves and panicking as the clock ticks down, while a computerised board shows the rapidly changing state of play. Russia's Alexander Grischuk won the crown, but the position illustrated was the most eye-catching game for tens of thousands of internet fans. India's Anand is the world number one but Radjabov, 20, is a fast-rising talent.

The young star caught his rival in a tricky variant of the Sicilian Poisoned Pawn and aimed to gun down the black king in mid-board. It seemed that White had overreached when they got to this diagram where White's two knights and his h4 bishop are all simultaneously attacked. Radjabov had it worked out, though.

What was his next winning move which forced Anand to resign?

David Buckley vs. Chris Shepherd

Bristol vs. Warwickshire, UK 4NCL league 2006.

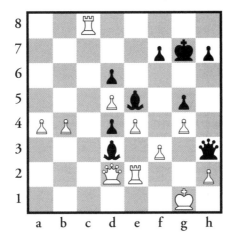

On the chess value scale a rook counts as the equivalent of five pawns, a bishop as three. So White should be in control here, with two rooks plus two extra pawns against Black's bishop pair. And the icing on White's cake is that he threatens instant checkmate by Qxg5. Yet despite all these assets, the position is totally winning for Black (to play)! Warwickshire expert Shepherd's next turn clinched victory, forcing the Bristol man's resignation.

What was Black's winning move?

PUZZLE 41 Viorel Bologan vs. Rafael Vaganian

European Club Cup, Fuegen 2006.

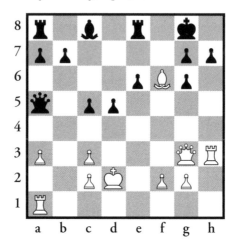

Grandmasters know that grabbing pawns while several pieces remain undeveloped is a likely route to a zero on the tournament chart. It still occurs, and there's usually a special reason. This game opened with a French Defence 1 e4 e6 where in the earlier moves Vaganian's knight pair raided the white camp and eliminated bishop, knight and three pawns before being shot down. Meanwhile, Bologan's queen, rook and bishop edged towards the black king and now White is ready to launch a decisive attack.

What was White's winning move?

Vassily Ivanchuk vs. Ivan Sokolov

European Club Cup 2006.

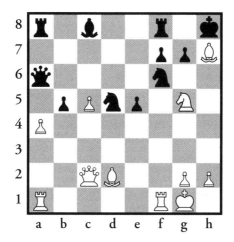

It's a classical formation known to every attacking player. The white queen combines with a knight at g5 or with a bishop on the b1-h7 diagonal to launch a checkmate attack on the black king holed up at g8 or h8. The paradoxical problem in this puzzle is that White has too many plausible options. Ukraine's world top ten grandmaster Ivanchuk would like to eliminate Sokolov's defensive f6 knight to enable Qh7 mate, but the knight is guarded by its partner at d5 so that, for example, 1 Rxf6 falls foul of Nxf6. And spectacular alternatives like 1 Bg8 and 1 Nxf7+ which sometimes solve such positions are also ineffective here. Ivanchuk saw through the confusing variety of choice. After his next turn, Black resigned.

What was White's winning move?

Daniel Gormally vs. Chris Ward

British rapidplay, Halifax 2001.

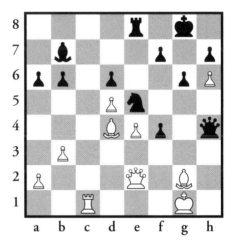

This encounter between two Kent grandmasters shows the power of a knight on a central square, plus a useful tactical pattern. Black's e5 horse cannot be dislodged by a white pawn, and is ready to join the queen in an attack on White's g1 king which lacks pawn cover. The knight can go to g4 to assist Qh2+, but Ward (Black, to move) visualised a subtler tactic based on the knight's control of f3. Few average players would consider this option since the f3 square seems well guarded by White's e2 queen and g2 bishop. Former British champion Ward conjured up a winning plan, and took just one turn to induce Gormally to resign.

What happened?

Lausanne 2003.

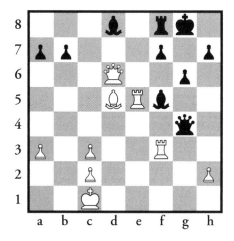

McShane and Bacrot, both 25, are the leading young talents of England and France, so this was a needle match. Black threatens Qxf1+, but White found a move to force resignation.

What happened?

European championship, Silivri 2003.

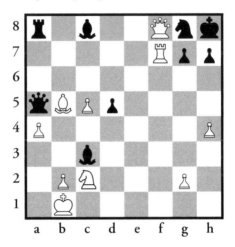

England's 25-year-old talent McShane features again, and this time it's a messy position with pieces scattered round the board. Moreover White (to play) is a bishop down. But the black king is vulnerable and his queen lacks squares, and it took just one turn to force Minasian's surrender.

Can you spot the finish?

Shakhriyar Mamedyarov vs. Benik Galstian

European U18 championship 2002.

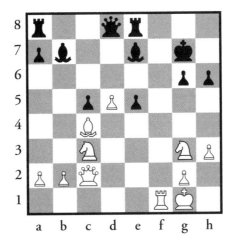

Azerbaijan, where all-time No. 1 Garry Kasparov learnt his skills, now has a whole generation of talented youngsters, and the white player here is ranked in the world top twenty grandmasters. Mamedyarov's pieces target the black king which is bereft of defenders and one move now forced resignation.

What was White's winner, and why did Black give up?

Monaco 2003.

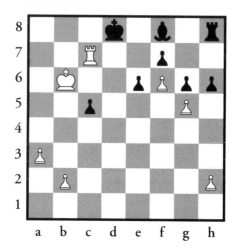

Two key aims of endgame play are to establish your rook on the seventh rank where it hems in the enemy king on the back row, and to use your own king as an active fighting piece. World champion Kramnik has achieved both goals here. He's a bishop down, but after his next turn Topalov resigned a hopeless position.

What happened?

Israeli championship 2003.

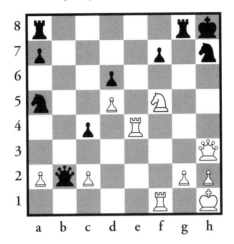

Israeli grandmaster Sutovsky is a musician, and when he won the 2001 European championship he sang his country's anthem in a fine baritone voice at the medal ceremony. Here his queen and rooks are targeted on Smirin's king and one move sufficed to end the game.

What was the winner?

Sydney 1934.

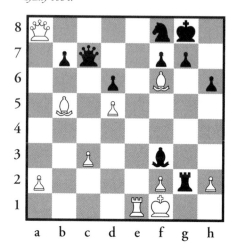

This old position gained a place in Australian chess folklore as a supreme example of setting a trap only for the trapper to find he had plotted his own downfall. Crowl's obvious choice is Rxh2.

Why is that a mistake, and can you find his actual move which forced Bunyan to surrender?

Jan Smeets vs. Marnus Carlsen

Corus Wijk aan Zee 2006.

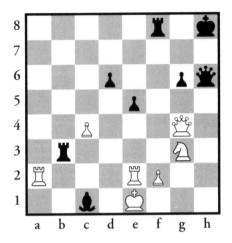

Norway's 18-year-old prodigy Carlsen was joint winner of the B group here at age 15, and his dynamic attacking play made him the hero of the spectators. Carlsen has already broken Bobby Fischer's age record as the youngest ever world title candidate, and he is now the world number four. Here his Dutch opponent is hanging on in a lost position two pawns down, but Carlsen's queen, rook and bishop all menace the exposed white king from a variety of angles. It took just one turn for the teenager to force resignation.

What was Black's winning move?

Ivan Cheparinov vs. Zoltan Almasi

Corus Wijk aan Zee B 2006.

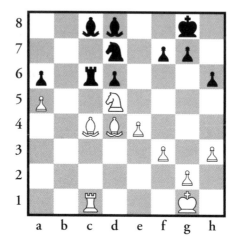

The B tournament winner was guaranteed a place in the 2007 elite group, although everybody knew that Norway's hugely talented Magnus Carlsen, then 15, would be promoted anyway to satisfy public clamour. The prodigy swapped the lead for several rounds with Russia's Alex Motylev, but Almasi seemed to have timed it right when he defeated Motylev in the penultimate round to take a half point lead. All the Hungarian needed was a draw with Black against his much lower ranked opponent. But it's well known that aiming only not to lose can be dangerously passive, and that's what happened here where the black army is corralled on the back rows, struggling to contain White's active pieces. Just one move sufficed to end Almasi's dreams and ensure that Motylev and Carlsen were promoted.

What happened?

PUZZLE 52 **Alexander Koblentz vs. Oleg Moiseev**

Latvia vs. Russia 1985.

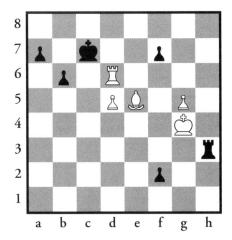

It looks hopeless for Black (to move). His rook is attacked, and if he queens his pawn White will win it by Rf6+ discovering check by the e5 bishop. But Moiseev found an imaginative resource, and next move it was White who had to resign.

What happened?

Copenhagen 2003.

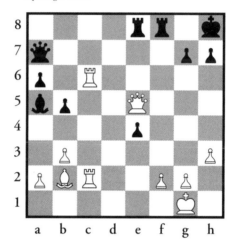

Queen and bishop lined up on the long diagonal plus rooks doubled on an open file spells trouble for a defender, but Black's position appears solid and he threatens Rxe5. Surprisingly, it took the Indian grandmaster (to play) just one move to induce the Russian to resign.

Can you spot the winning move, and explain Black's surrender?

Goran Todorevic vs. Jesse Kraai

Budapest 2003.

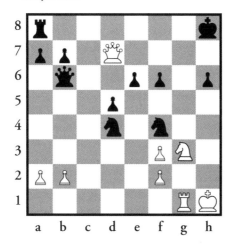

Black is a knight and two pawns ahead, yet White (to play) found a surprise counter, exploiting Black's g7 and h7 weak points, against which there is no defence.

Can you spot White's winner?

Ivan Sokolov vs. Artashes Minasian

European Cup 1995.

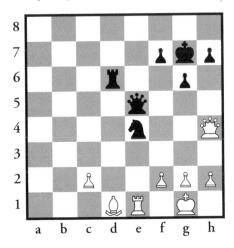

Black (to play) is a pawn down, but the key is White's castled king behind a trio of unmoved pawns.

Black uses the back rank theme to force White's resignation in just one move.

Carl Schlechter vs. Phillip Meitner

Vienna 1899.

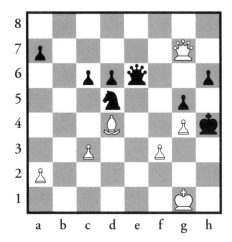

White appears in a difficult position. Black, who is a pawn up, controls the central squares with queen and knight. But the black king is in an exposed situation at h4, and Schlechter (to play) found a brilliant winning move to force checkmate.

What happened?

Emil Schallopp vs. Max Weiss

Graz 1880.

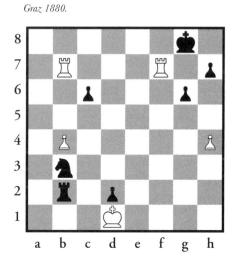

Black threatens to queen his pawn in only two moves by Rb1+ Kc2 d1Q+, so Schallopp decided to force a draw by 1 Rg7+ when the white rooks keep checking.

What did the masters overlook?

Nikolai Polechuk vs. Igor Foigel

postal game 1981.

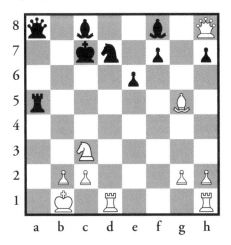

Foigel has only bishop for rook and pawn, but he threatens immediate checkmate by Ra1. Game over? Indeed it was, as White (to play) found a move which forced Black's immediate resignation.

What happened?

Yuri Razuvaev vs. Joszef Kling

Palma 1989.

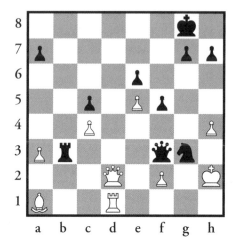

A perfect example of a position where whoever moves first wins. Given the chance, White will checkmate by Qd8+, Rd7+ and Qg5 mate, but Black (to play) finds a move of his own which leads to inescapable mate.

Federico Manca vs. Ferdinand Braga

Reggio Emilia 1992.

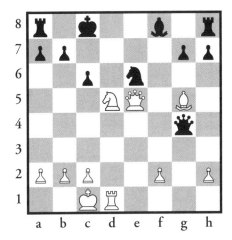

Most chessplayers would agree that the game is more competitive sport than creative art, yet there is still a frisson of elation when you launch an imaginative attack and sacrifice material just on a speculative hunch that there will be a winning tactic at the end. Here White (to play) has given up a whole rook, expecting compensation in threats to the black king while the defender's rooks and bishop are stranded. Black had an earlier chance to refute White's concept, but preferred this diagram where he threatens both Qxg5+ and cxd5.

What was White's winning move?

Tim Kras vs. Van Easton

Philadelphia 1992.

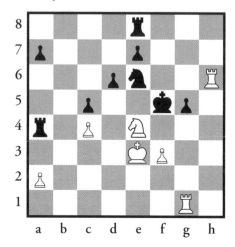

If you are down on material, try to generate threats to your opponent's king. Here White (to play) has a two-pawn deficit but found a way to catch the black monarch in mid-board.

What happened?

David Janowski vs. Carl Schlechter

London 1899.

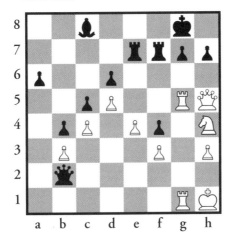

White (to play) forced checkmate with such an impressive move that they called it *The pearl of St Stephen's* after the London hall where the tournament was played.

Can you find White's elegant finish?

Oleg Dashkanov vs. Artur Yusupov
Moscow 1981.

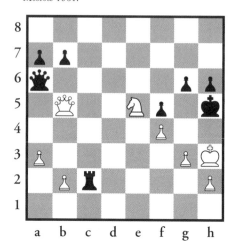

White was an unknown, Black a grandmaster and later world semi-finalist. So Dashkanov naturally got outplayed until this position where he saw that avoiding a queen exchange would allow Qf1 mate. White resigned, and Yusupov looked relieved.

Why?

Lajos Portisch vs. Viktor Korchnoi

Amsterdam 1980.

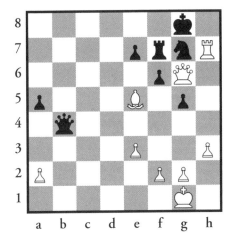

Chess legend Korchnoi had a lost game, but still hoped for a trap. If White plays the obvious 1 Qh6, threatening 2 Qh8 mate, Black has the long distance check Qb1+! and Qxh7 winning. Backward threats by queen or bishop are the easiest to overlook. Portisch kept cool, though.

What was White's winning move?

Erich Joppen vs. Robert Wade

Amsterdam 1954.

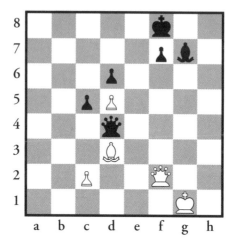

In the old days unfinished games used to be adjourned overnight, and in this position from an England vs. Germany match, Black (to play) is a pawn up. The England team analysed for several hours and came up with 1...c4, which next morning led to a draw. Afterwards the Germans revealed Black's winner which they had spotted in seconds.

What should Black have played?

Martin Martens vs. Jeroen Piket

Eindhoven 1993.

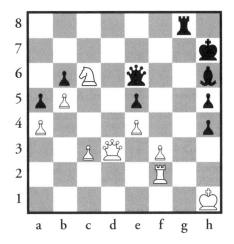

Piket, No. 2 Netherlands grandmaster at the time, plans a checkmate attack here, but the obvious play 1…Qh3+ 2 Rh2 Qg3 allows White to start an unclear checking series by 3 Qd7+. Black's much better move in the diagram proved so strong that White immediately resigned.

What happened?

Alexei Shirov vs. Vishy Anand

Monaco 1998.

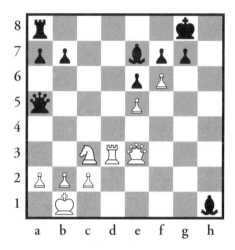

White (to move) is a bishop down. He can regain it by 1 fxe7, but then Re8 and Black holds on. Shirov made a much stronger move, and when Anand realised its implications he decided to resign.

What was the winner which induced Black's surrender?

Salo Flohr vs. Rudolf Spielmann

Bled 1931.

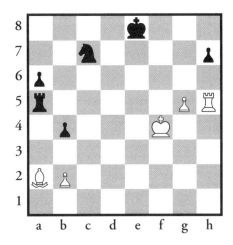

The game was a clash of generations and a contrast in styles. The subtle strategies of Flohr, 23, made him the most talented young grandmaster in Europe, while Spielmann, 48, was a dashing attacker who had made his name with the old-style King's Gambit 1 e4 e5 2 f4. Their hard-fought encounter reached this endgame where Spielmann is a pawn up but Flohr (White, to move) has the obvious possibility of 1 Rxh7 Rxa2 2 Rxc7 Rxb2 3 g6 Rg2. It is then a tricky rook ending, so White looked at other possibilities such as 1 Bb1 menacing the h7 pawn but allowing Ne6+ and Nxg5 giving up Black's knight for the last white pawn. White would then have chances to reach rook, and bishop against rook which is a theoretical draw though with practical winning chances. A tough decision, but Flohr made the right move in the diagram and Spielmann resigned immediately.

What happened?

Mikhail Tal vs. Cathy Forbes

Chicago 1988.

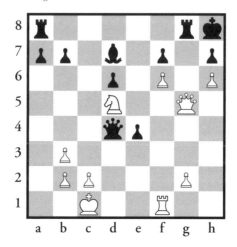

Londoner Forbes has a unique record in chess history. The England international was Bobby Fischer's opponent in the only recorded game the American legend played against a woman, a friendly encounter during Fischer's controversial 1992 rematch against Boris Spassky in the former Yugoslavia. Fischer, who once famously boasted that he could give any female opponent a knight start, paid Forbes the compliment of taking her on on level terms.

Less well-known is Forbes's game here against another chess immortal. Tal is widely reckoned the best attacking genius of all time, and he does not disappoint in this finish.

How does White (to play) win immediately?

John Carleton vs. Nigel Povah

North West Eagles vs. Guildford-ADC B, UK 4NCL League 2005.

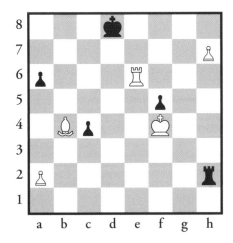

It is all too easy to slip up in the final moves of a winning endgame. Here White (to play) is bishop for pawn ahead, but his advanced h7 pawn is menaced by Black's h2 rook. A plausible sequence runs 1 Re7 c3! 2 Bxc3 Kxe7 3 h8Q Rxh8 4 Bxh8 Kc8 5 Kxf5. Now White is a full bishop ahead, but the game is drawn because the bishop does not control a8, the queening square for the white a pawn. Black simply parks his king at a8, from where it can never be dislodged.

Can you find White's winning move?

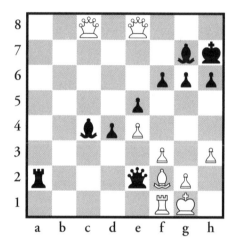

What's the difference between a master and a grandmaster? This position was published in *Chess* magazine some years ago, and submitted to a panel of masters for their verdict. White (to move) has two queens on the board, one a promoted pawn. He is queen for bishop and pawn ahead, but Black has the powerful threat of Qxf1+ and Qxf2, while 1 Re1? loses immediately to Qxf2+ and Qxg2 mate.

In the actual game, White gave up queen for bishop by 1 Qxc4, and the entire master panel agreed that this concession was forced. But the panel had one grandmaster member, GM John Nunn, and he was a lone dissenter, arguing that White is actually winning in the diagram.

What did the grandmaster spot that the masters missed?

Michael Adams vs. Garry Kasparov

Linares 2005.

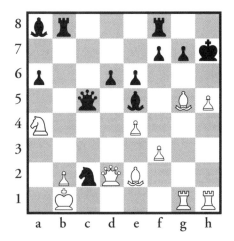

This was the final stage of Kasparov's last great game before announcing his retirement. The all-time number one had launched a fierce attack on the Cornishman's king. Black's strike force of queen, rook, bishop and knight should be sufficient, but Adams still hoped to escape since he threatens both Nxc5 and Qxc2. If Black tries Na3+, then White answers Ka2 with a possible draw by Nc2 Kb1 with repeated position. Kasparov had everything accurately planned, and his next turn induced the England number one's resignation.

What was Black's winning move?

Miso Cebalo vs. Vlad Tkachiev

Rabac 2003.

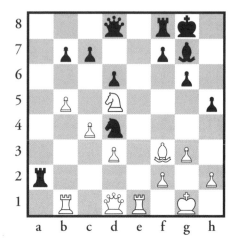

Tkachiev, 35, has been designated the hunk of world chess. The former Kazak grandmaster, who has since represented both France and Russia, describes his offboard pleasures as "sea, sangria and sex" and is a specialist in blitz chess, where players have five minutes or less for all moves. One of his unorthodox tips for when both sides are short of time on the clock is to try to steer the action towards your hand that moves the pieces and presses the clock button. Chess rules say that the same hand has to be used for both actions. Tkachiv has a sharp tactical eye, and here as Black (to move) he forced his Croatian opponent to resign in just one move from the diagram.

Can you find the finish?

Alex Grischuk vs. Alex Morozevich

Dubai 2002.

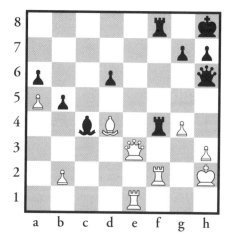

Grischuk, 25, is the rising hope of Russian chess while Morozevich, 31, is well established in the elite. Both have designs on the world title and both are sharp tacticians, so their games against each other often feature risky play of a type shown in the diagram.

Moro has just captured Grischuk's f4 pawn, reckoning that after 1 Rxf4 Qxf4+ 2 Qxf4 Rxf4 3 Re8+ Bg8 there is no checkmate while Black has an extra pawn. Even then, bishops of opposite colours (the white bishop operates on dark squares, Black's on light) would probably lead to a draw, but Moro had missed something in his calculations.

With White to move, how did the game end?

Ewfim Geller vs. Evgeny Sveshnikov

USSR championship, Tbilisi 1978.

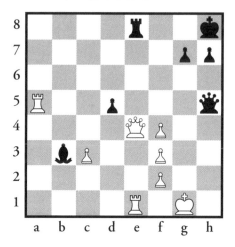

Geller was a star of his generation, several times a world-title candidate
and with a plus score against Bobby Fischer. He launched new ideas in
his favourite King's Indian (1 d4 Nf6 2 c4 g6 3 Nc3 Bg7) and worked all
night to save the then world champion Mikhail Botvinnik from defeat in his
only game with Fischer. Older players are prone to tactical oversights, and
Geller made a big one in the puzzle illustrated. Yet a year later he came
back to win the competitive USSR title at age 54. Here White's last turn
Rb1-e1 was clever, planning dxe4 Rxh5 when White wins on material, or
Rxe4 Ra8+! Re8 Rxe8+ Qxe8 Rxe8 mate. Sveshnikov, then an unknown
but since inventor of a fashionable Sicilian Defence line named after him,
spotted the flaw in Geller's thinking and forced immediate resignation.

What was Black's knock-out punch?

Evgeny Bareev vs. Arkady Naiditsch

European Club Cup 2003.

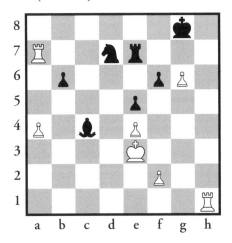

Chess primers tell you that the rook (five points) and pawn (one point) are worth about the same as bishop and knight (three points each) but don't you believe it. Unless the extra pawn is far advanced *en route* to queen, in practice the nimble lone rook usually lords it over the prelate and horse, which are not natural co-workers. In this example an experienced world-top-20 Russian has the rook, and Germany's best young grandmaster the bishop/knight duo. No contest. Just one move sufficed for Bareev to force resignation.

How did it end?

Viorel Bologan vs. Joel Lautier

Wood Green vs. Guildford-ADC, UK 4NCL league 2005.

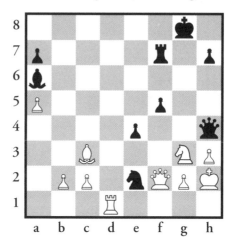

The two London area teams completely dominated the national league, each winning ten matches before meeting in the final round. Barbican, representing City of London amateurs, finished an excellent third. League rules allow wildcard additions, so both Wood Green and Guildford-ADC flew in highly ranked grandmasters from all over Europe for the showdown. On top board, England number one Michael Adams drew with four-time Russian champion Peter Svidler. Lower down, the champions of Moldova and France met in what turned out to be the league title decider.

Bologan (White, to play) is a pawn up but looks in trouble against Black's threatening king's side army. White had calculated well, spotting a tactical setpiece against the black king. Just one move in the diagram settled the game and the UK league championship.

What happened?

Judit Polgar vs. Shakhriyar Mamedyarov

Bled Olympiad 2002.

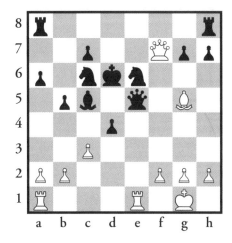

Polgar is the first woman to compete in an elite world championship against men. The Hungarian, 31, has taken two motherhood breaks but returned to the grandmaster circuit with impressive results. Here her sacrificial attacking play has gambited both knights to catch the black king in mid-board. Mamedyarov hopes for the obvious 1 Rxe5 Nxe5 2 Q or Be7+ Kd5 with chances to survive the attack. Polgar's actual move was stronger and forced immediate resignation.

What happened?

Vishy Anand vs. Ye Jiangchuan

Asian team championship, Kuala Lumpur 1989.

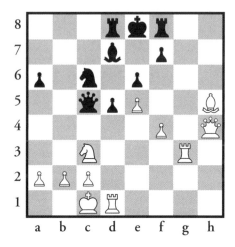

Some 1,400 years ago India and China were the seedbeds of chess, although China had its own version with different rules. When the game developed internationally in the 19th century, the two Asian countries remained backwaters with little or no participation. All that has changed radically in the past 20 years. The emergence of Anand as a world-title contender inspired India, while the Chinese government officially promoted the game. Now Anand is world number one, while China consistently wins gold at the biennial women's Olympiads and has many talented juniors. Asian team contests are usually decided by the India vs. China result, and here Anand (White, to play) is a pawn up while his pieces probe Black's defences from several directions. One move was enough to cause a rapid collapse of Jiangchuan's fortress.

What happened?

Veselin Topalov vs. Garry Kasparov

match 1998.

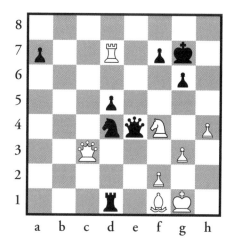

Even when a bishop down as here, Kasparov remains dangerous. Topalov can win by 1 Kh2! when the obvious Rxf1 loses to 2 Qxd4+! Qxd4 3 Ne6+ and 4 Nxd4 with a knight for two pawns. Topalov thought he had an easier win, so played 1 Rxd5.

What did he miss?

The Solutions

Sir George Thomas vs. Alfred Brinckmann

Budapest 1929.

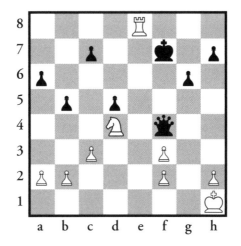

1 Rf8+! Kxf8 2 Ne6+ and 3 Nxf4 wins.

Aleksei Alexandrov vs. Alexey Lusto

Elista 1998.

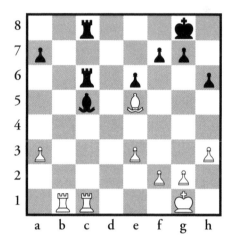

1 Rb8! If Rxb8 2 Bxb8 and 3 Bxa7 gains material. If Kh7 2 Rxc8 Rxc8 3 Bd4.

David Bronstein vs. Grigory Levenfish

USSR championship 1946.

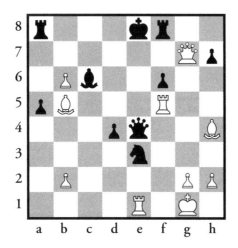

1 Re5+! and if fxe5 2 Qe7 mate, or Qxe5 2 Bxc6+ Kd8 3 Qd7 mate, or
Kd8 2 Qc7 mate.

Reuben Fine vs. Herman Steiner

Hollywood 1945.

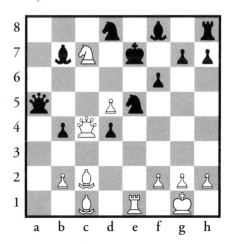

1 d6+! Resigns. If Kxd6 (or Kd7 2 Bf5+ wins) 2 Nb5+ Kd7 3 Bf5+ Ne6 4 Qxe6+ Kd8 5 Rxe5 fxe5 6 Qd7 mate.

USSR championship 1954.

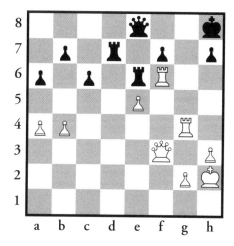

1 Qf4! Resigns. If Rxe5 2 Qh6 mates or wins the queen, Rxf6 2 Qxf6 mates, while Qf8 2 Rxe6 wins a rook since fxe6 allows 3 Qxf8 mate.

Olaf Barda vs. Jan Foltys

Marianske Lazne 1951.

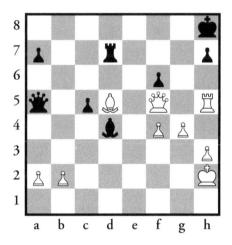

1 Rxh7+! Rxh7 2 Qc8+ Kg7 3 Qg8+ Kh6 4 g5+ and mate by fxg5 5 Qxg5 or Kh5 5 Qxh7.

David Bronstein vs. Alexander Kotov

Moscow championship 1946.

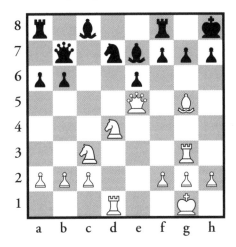

1 Bh6! Resigns. If Nxe5 2 Bxg7+ Kg8 3 Bxe5+ Bg5 4 Rxg5 mate.

Olot 1971.

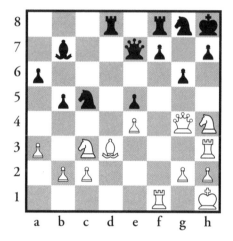

1 Rxf7! Qxf7 2 Nxg6+ Kg7 3 Nxe5+ wins the queen.

Etienne Bacrot vs. Lother Vogt

Arusa 1996.

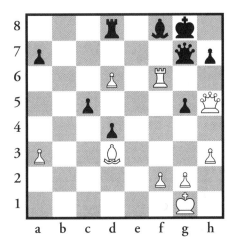

1 Rg6! hxg6 2 Bc4+ wins.

Southsea 1950.

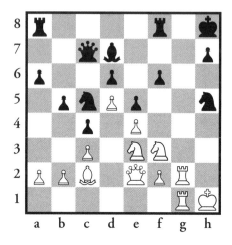

1 Nxe5! Nf4? (better fxe5 2 Qxh5 but then White is a clear pawn up) 2 Rg8+! Rxg8 3 Nf7 mate.

Dibyendu Barua vs. Viktor Korchnoi

Lloyds Bank London 1982.

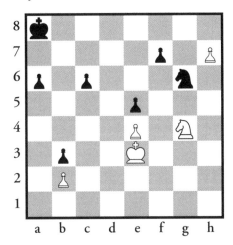

1 Nxe5! Nh8 2 Nxf7! Nxf7 3 e5! and Korchnoi resigned. White will queen a pawn.

Ulf Andersson vs. Bengt Horberg

Swedish championship 1969.

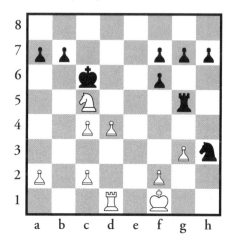

1 d5+! If Kxc5 2 d6 and White's pawn queens. If Kd6 2 Ne4+ forks king and rook.

London 1851.

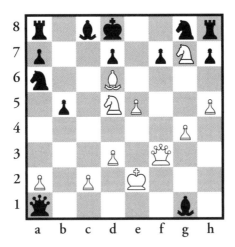

1 Qf6+! Nxf6 2 Be7 mate.

Dr James Aitken vs. Roland Payne

British championship, Whitby 1962.

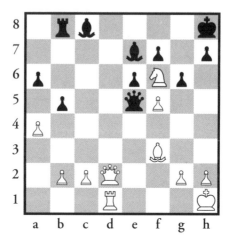

1 Qh6! Resigns. If Qxf6 2 Rd8+! Bxd8 3 Qf8 mate.

Bognor 1963.

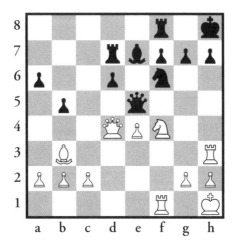

1 Bxf7! Resigns. If Qxd4 2 Ng6 mate. If Rxf7 2 Ng6+ and 3 Nxe5 wins the queen.

Peter Leko vs. Lazaro Bruzon

Corus Wijk aan Zee 2005.

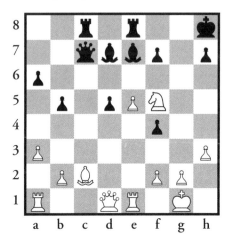

1 e6! Resigns. If fxe6 2 Qd4+ e5 (Kg8 3 Qg7 mate) 3 Rxe5 Bf6 4 Rxe8+ wins. If Bxe6 2 Qd4+ f6 3 Rxe6 wins.

European championship, Warsaw 2005.

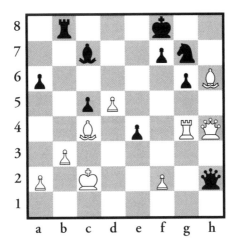

1 Qf6! Qxh6 and now the amateurs saw 2 Rh4 Nh5 which favours Black, but White planned instead 2 d6! with the winning double threat of 3 Qxf7 mate and 3 dxc7. If 2...Ne6 2 Bxe6 and White keeps both threats.

Luke McShane vs. Branko Damljanovic

England vs. Serbia, European team championship, Gothenburg 2005.

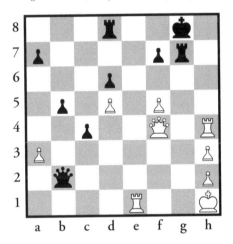

1 Rh8+! Kxh8 2 Qh4+ and if Kg8 3 Qxd8+ Kh7 4 Qh4+ Kg8 5 Re8 mate or Rh7 3 Qxd8+ Kg7 4 Rg1+ Kh6 5 Qh4 mate.

Stewart Haslinger vs. Michael Waters

Smith & Williamson British Championship, Douglas 2005.

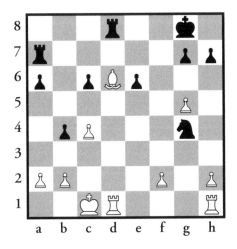

1 f3! Resigns. The point is Nf2 2 Bc5! Rxd1+ 3 Rxd1 Nxd1 (if Rf7 4 Rd8+ Rf8 5 Rxf8 mate or Rd7 4 Bxf2) 4 Bxa7 and Black's knight is trapped and lost.

Bratislava 1993.

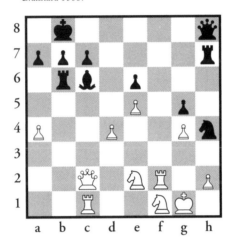

1 Qxh7! Resigns. If Qxh7 2 Rf8+ Be8 3 Rxe8 mate.

ANSWER 21 Emanuel Berg vs. Evgeny Bareev

European team championship, Gothenburg 2005.

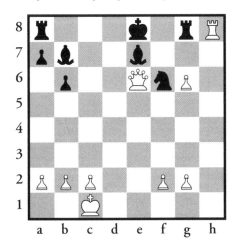

1 g7 Resigns. The threat is 2 Rxg8 Nxg8 3 Qxg8+ Kd7 4 Qxa8 Bxa8 5 g8Q. If Bd5 2 Rxg8+ Nxg8 3 Qxd5 Rd8 4 Qxg8+ Kd7 5 Qxd8+ Bxd8 6 g8Q wins.

Andras Adorjan vs. Anatoly Karpov

Hoogeveen 2003.

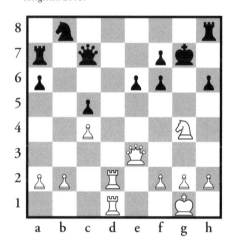

1 Rd8! If Rxd8 2 Qxh6+ Kg8 3 Nxf6 mate. If Rh7 2 Qf3 f5 3 Qc3+ wins.

Buenos Aires 1942.

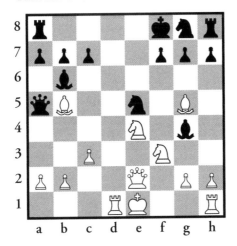

1 Nxe5! Bxe2 2 Nd7+ Ke8 3 Nb8+! c6 4 Nd6+ Kf8 5 Nd7 mate.

Max Dlugy vs. Stephen Stoyko

Cherry Hill 1991.

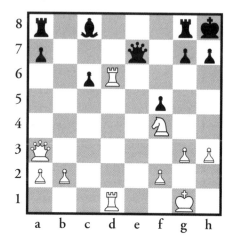

1 Rh6! and Black resigned because if Qxa3 2 Ng6 mate or gxh6 2 Qxe7.

Harry Golombek vs. Nicholas Rossolimo

Venice 1950.

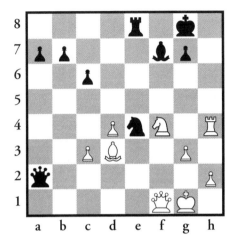

1 Ng6! (threat 2 Rh8 mate) Bxg6 2 Bc4+ wins the queen.

Rogelio Antonio vs. Dao Thein Hai

Malaysian Open 2005.

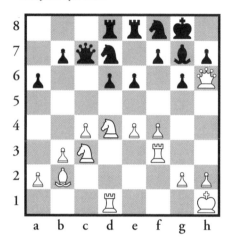

1 Qxg7+! Resigns. If Kxg7 2 Nd5! exd5 (else White regains the queen with a bishop ahead) 3 Nf5++ Kg8 4 Nh6 mate.

Bragi Thorfinsson vs. Amar Gunnarson

Reykjavik 2006.

1...Rxg2+! 2 Kh1 (if 2 Kxg2 Rg4++ 3 Kh2 Qg2 mate) Rh4! when if 3 Nxh4 Rxf2+ wins the f6 queen or 3 Qxh4 Rg4+ or 3 Qf7+ Rg7+! 4 f3 Rxh3 mate.

Hilversum 1947.

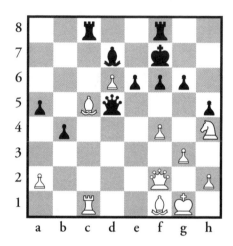

1 Qc2! (threat 2 Qxg6 mate) Rg8 2 Bg2 traps Black's queen.

World Cup, Khanty Mansiysk 2005.

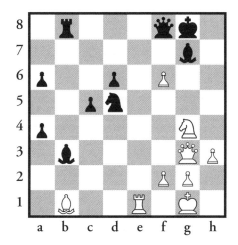

1 f7+! Resigns. If Qxf7 2 Nh6+ forks king and queen. If Kxf7 2 Nh6+ Bxh6 3 Qg6 mate.

World Cup 2005.

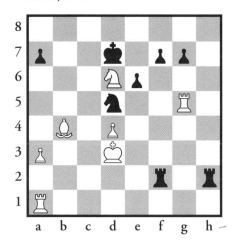

1...Rf3+ (or Rh3+) and if 2 Ke4 Re3 mate or 2 Kc4 Kc6! with the winning double threat Nb6 mate or Rc2+ Bc3 Rxc3 mate. If 3 Rxd5 exd5 mate.

Corus Wijk aan Zee 2006.

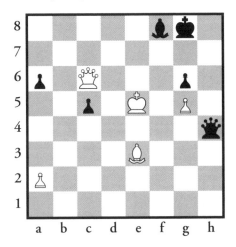

1...Qh8+! and White resigned. If 2 Kd5/e4 Qh1+ skewers king and queen. If 2 Kf4 Bd6+! when 3 Qxd6 Qh2+ wins the queen, 3 Ke4 again allows Qh1+xc6, while if 3 Kg4 Qh5 is checkmate. If 1...Qh8+ 2 Ke6 Qh3+! 3 Kd5 (3 Kf6/e5 Qf5 mate) Qh1+xc6 wins.

Helsinki 1932.

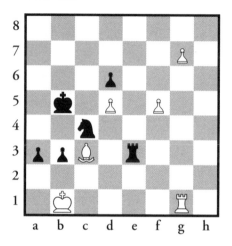

1...Rxc3! 2 g8Q Nd2+ 3 Ka1 Rc1+! 4 Rxc1 b2+ 5 Ka2 bxc1N+! 6 Kxa3 Nc4 mate. The rare promotion to knight set up the final checkmate.

Biel 1997.

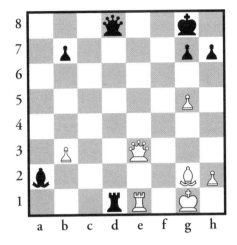

1 Bd5+! Resigns. If Qxd5 2 Qe8 mate, or Rxd5 2 Qe6+ Kh8 3 Qe8+ and mates.

Andre Lilienthal vs. Ivan Aramanovic

Moscow 1945.

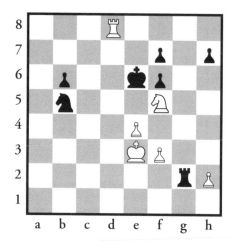

1 Rd5! and if Rb2 2 Rxb5 Rxb5 3 Nd4+ and 4 Nxb5 wins. If 1 Rd5 Na3 2 Rd6+ Ke5 3 f4 mate.

USSR Young Masters 1977.

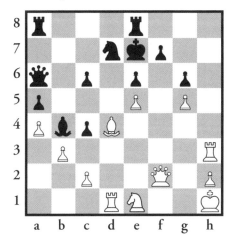

1 Qf6+! (1 Bc5+ Kd8 2 Rxd7+ also wins) Nxf6 2 Bc5+! Bxc5 3 gxf6+ Kf8
4 Rh8 mate.

Alusha 1998.

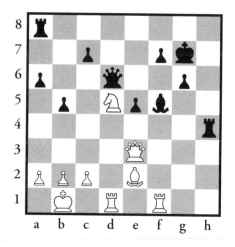

1 Rxf5! Resigns. If gxf5 2 Qg5+ wins the h4 rook.

Alexey Shirov vs. Alex Areschenko

Aerosvit Yalta 2006.

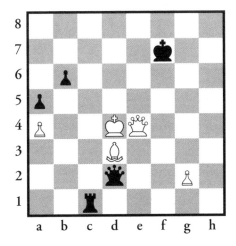

1...Rc4+! 2 Kxc4 Qb4+ 3 Kd5 Qc5 mate.

Experience vs. Youth, Amsterdam 2006.

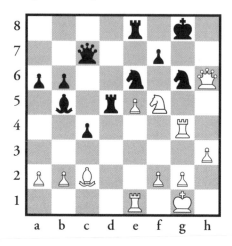

1 Rh4! Resigns. The threat is 2 Qh7+ Kf8 3 Qh8+ Nxh8 4 Rxh8 mate.
If Nxh4 2 Ne7+! Q or Rxe7 3 Qh7+ Kf8 4 Qh8 mate.

Teimour Radjabov vs. Vishy Anand

World Blitz Championship, Israel 2006.

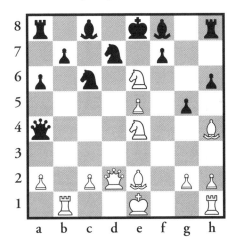

1 Nf6+! Resigns. If Nxf6 2 Nc7+ Ke7 3 Qd6 mate. If Ke7 2 Qd6 mate.

David Buckley vs. Chris Shepherd

Bristol vs. Warwickshire, UK 4NCL league 2006.

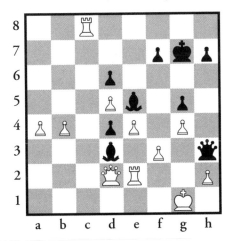

1...Bxh2+! and if 2 Rxh2 Qf1 mate or 2 Kf2 Qg3+ 3 Kf1 Qg1 mate.

Viorel Bologan vs. Rafael Vaganian

European Club Cup, Fuegen 2006.

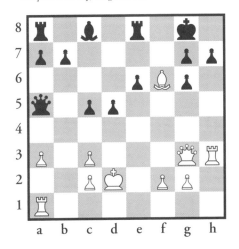

1 Rxh7! and Black resigned. If Kxh7 2 Rh1+ Kg8 3 Qxg6 Qc7 4 Qh7+ Kf8 5 Qh8+ Kf7 6 Qxg7 mate.

European Club Cup 2006.

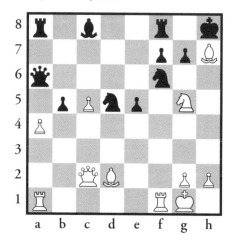

1 Be4! Resigns. White threatens 2 Bxd5 Nxd5 3 Qh7 mate. If Bb7 2 Bxd5 Bxd5 3 Rxf6! with the same mate threat. If g6 2 Bxd5 Nxd5 3 Qe4! Nf6 4 Rxf6 Qxf6 5 Qh4+ Kg7 6 Qh7 mate.

Daniel Gormally vs. Chris Ward

British rapidplay, Halifax 2001.

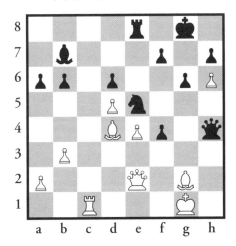

1...f3! 2 Bxf3 Qg5+ wins the c1 rook.

Luke McShane vs. Etienne Bacrot

Lausanne 2003.

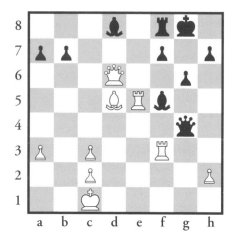

1 Rexf5! Resigns. If gxf5 2 Rg3 wins Black's queen.

Luke McShane vs. Artashes Minasian

European championship, Silivri 2003.

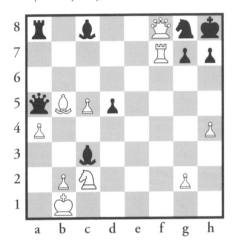

1 b4! when if Bxb4 2 Qxg7 mate.

Shakhriyar Mamedyarov vs. Benik Galstian

European U18 championship 2002.

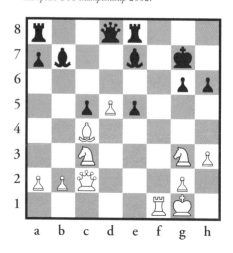

1 Nh5+! gxh5 2 Rf7+! Kxf7 3 Qh7+ Kf8 (if Kf6 4 Ne4 mate) 4 d6 with Qf7 or Qg8 mate.

Vlad Kramnik vs. Veselin Topalov

Monaco 2003.

1 Kc6! Resigns. The threat is 2 Ra7 and 3 Ra8 mate. If 1…Bd6 2 Kxd6
Re8 3 Ra7 Kc8 4 Ra8+ Kb7 5 Rxe8 wins.

Israeli championship 2003.

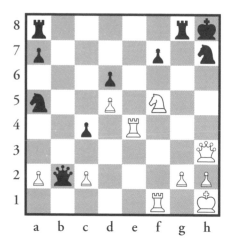

1 Qxh7+! Kxh7 2 Rh4+ Kg6 3 Rh6+ Kg5 4 h4+ Kg4 5 Ne3+ Kg3 6 Rf3 mate.

Alex Bunyan vs. Frank Crowl

Sydney 1934.

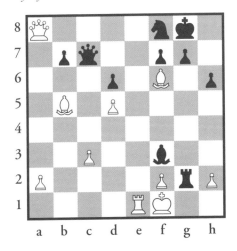

Bunyan's trap was 1...Rxh2? 2 Qxf8+! Kxf8 3 Re8 mate. Crowl played 1...Qc4+! 2 Bxc4 Rxh2 and White resigned as Rh1 mate can only be stopped by ruinous sacrifices.

Jan Smeets vs. Marnus Carlsen

Corus Wijk aan Zee 2006.

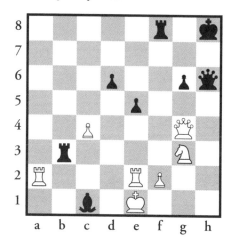

1...Rxg3! and White resigned because of 2 fxg3/Qxg3 Qh1+ forcing checkmate.

Ivan Cheparinov vs. Zoltan Almasi

Corus Wijk aan Zee B 2006.

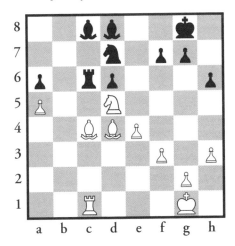

1 Ne7+! Resigns. If Bxe7 2 Bxf7+! Kxf7 3 Rxc6 Bb7 4 Re7 wins the b7 bishop or the d7 knight to guarantee White an easy material win.

Alexander Koblentz vs. Oleg Moiseev

Latvia vs. Russia 1985.

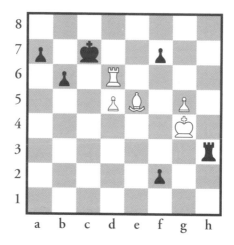

1…f5+! 2 exf6 en passant f1Q and White's rook cannot discover an attack on the new queen. White therefore resigned.

Krishnan Sasikiran vs. Konstantin Sakaev

Copenhagen 2003.

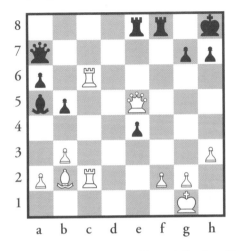

1 Rxa6! Resigns. If Qxa6 2 Qxg7 mate. If Rxe5 2 Rxa7 and White wins the e5 rook or the a5 bishop.

Budapest 2003.

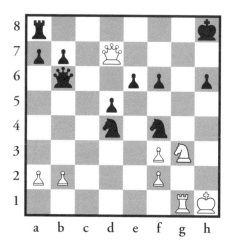

1 Ne4! (threat 2 Qg7 mate) Rg8 2 Qh7+! Kxh7 3 Nxf6+ Kh8 4 Rxg8 mate.

European Cup 1995.

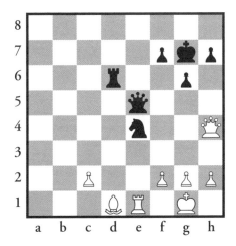

1... Nc3! and White resigned. If 2 Rxe5 Rxd1+ mates, or 2 Rf1 Rxd1 wins a bishop.

Vienna 1899.

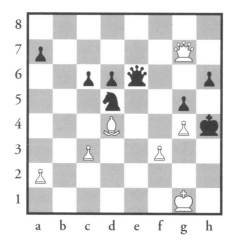

1 Qxh6+! Qxh6 2 Kh2 and White mates by Bf2.

Graz 1880.

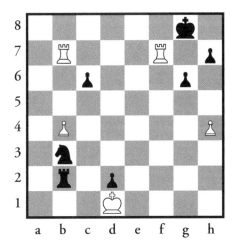

White can allow Black a new queen because of 1 Rfd7! Rb1+ 2 Kc2 Rc1+ 3 Kb2 d1Q 4 Rb8 mate.

Nikolai Polechuk vs. Igor Foigel

postal game 1981.

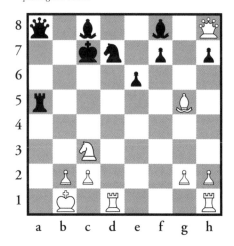

1 Qxh6+! Qxh6 2 Kh2 and White mates by Bf2.

Yuri Razuvaev vs. Joszef Kling

Palma 1989.

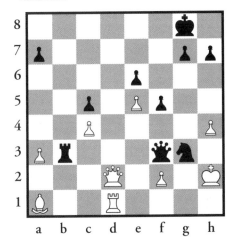

1...Nf1+ 2 Rxf1 Qh3+ 3 Kg1 Qg4+ 4 Kh2 Rh3 mate.

Federico Manca vs. Ferdinand Braga

Reggio Emilia 1992.

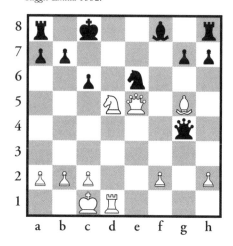

1 Qc7+! Nxc7 2 Nb6+ axb6 3 Rd8 mate.

Tim Kras vs. Van Easton

Philadelphia 1992.

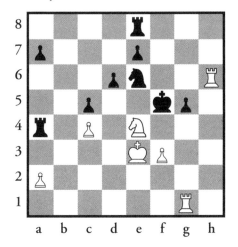

1 Rxg5+! Nxg5 2 Ng3+ Ke5 3 f4 mate.

David Janowski vs. Carl Schlechter

London 1899.

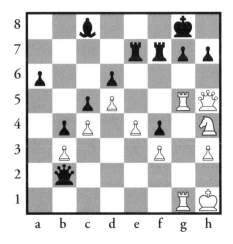

1 Qxh7+! Kxh7 2 Rh5+ Kg8 3 Ng6 Rf6 4 Rh8+ Kf7 5 Rf8 mate.

Moscow 1981.

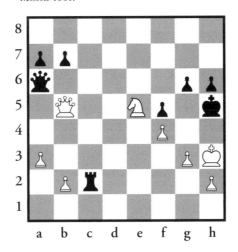

1 g4+ fxg4 2 Nxg4+ forces checkmate. If Qxb5 3 Nf6 mate or 2...g5 3 Qe8+ Qg6 4 Nf6 mate.

Amsterdam 1980.

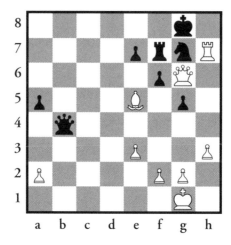

1 Kh2! and Black resigned. The main threat is 2 Qh6 and 3 Rh8 mate. Portisch's king move means that Black has no longer has the checking Qb1 as a defence.

Amsterdam 1954.

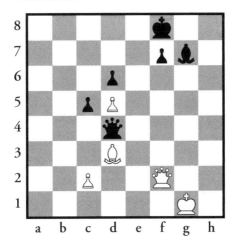

Simply 1...Qxd3! 2 cxd3 Bd4 forces a winning pawn endgame.

Eindhoven 1993.

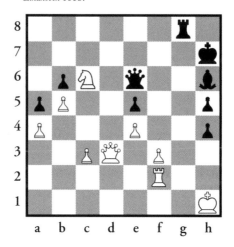

1...Be3! and White resigned. If 2 Rh2 Rg1 mate. If 2 Qxe3 Qh3+ 3 Rh2 Qf1+ 4 Qg1 Qxg1 mate.

Monaco 1998.

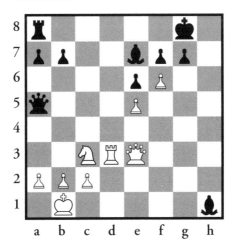

1 Qg1! and Black resigned. If Bf8 (to stop 2 Qxg7 mate) 2 Rg3 g6 3 Rxg6+ fxg6 4 Qxg6+ Kh8 5 f7 (threat 6 Qg8 mate) Bg7 6 Qh5+ Bh6 7 Qxh6 mate.

Salo Flohr vs. Rudolf Spielmann

Bled 1931.

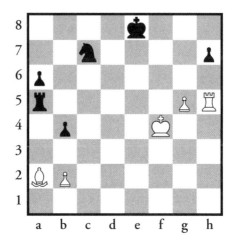

1 g6! Resigns. If Rxh5 2 g7 and White queens his pawn. If 1…hxg6 2 Rxa5 wins.

Mikhail Tal vs. Cathy Forbes

Chicago 1988.

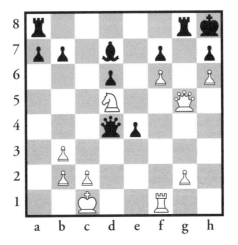

1 Qg7+! Rxg7 2 hxg7+ Kg8 3 Ne7 mate.

John Carleton vs. Nigel Povah

North West Eagles vs. Guildford-ADC B, UK 4NCL League 2005.

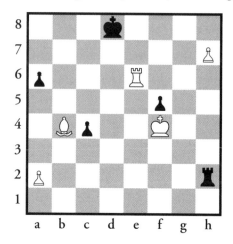

1 Rxa6! Rxh7 2 Ra8+ Kd7 3 Ra7+ and 4 Rxh7 wins.

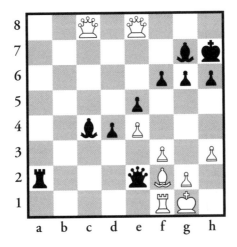

1 Qg4! Qxf1+ 2 Kh2 (threat 3 Qgxg6 mate) g5 3 Qf5 mate.

Linares 2005.

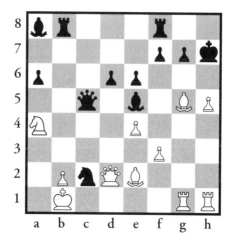

1 Qxh6+! Qxh6 2 Kh2 and White mates by Bf2. 1…Qa3! and White resigned. The threat is Rxb2+ Nxb2 Qxb2 mate. If 2 Kxc2 Qxa4+ 3 Kd3 Qd4+ 4 Kc2 Rxb2+ wins. So White's only try is 2 Qxc2 Rfc8 when if 3 Qd2 Qxa4 or 3 Qxc8 (hoping for Rxc8 4 bxa3) Rb2+! 4 Nxb2 Qxb2 mate.

Miso Cebalo vs. Vlad Tkachiev

Rabac 2003.

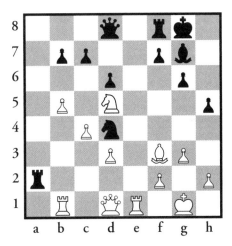

1...Rd2! and White resigned. If 2 Qxd2 Nxf3+ and Nxd2 wins the queen.

Dubai 2002.

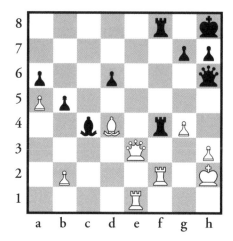

1 Kg3! wins. If Rxf2 2 Qxh6 and the black g7 pawn is pinned by the bishop so cannot recapture. The game ended 1 Kg3 Qg5 2 Rxf4 and Black resigned.

USSR championship, Tbilisi 1978.

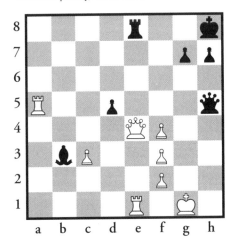

1...Qg6+! and White resigned. If 2 Qxg6 Rxe1+ 3 Kg2 hxg6 and Black has bishop for pawn with a simple win on material.

Evgeny Bareev vs. Arkady Naiditsch

European Club Cup 2003.

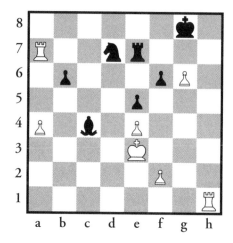

1 Rh7! Resigns. White wins knight or rook.

Viorel Bologan vs. Joel Lautier

Wood Green vs. Guildford-ADC, UK 4NCL league 2005.

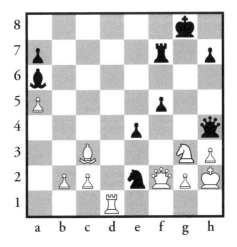

1 Nxf5! Resigns. If Qxf2 2 Rd8+ Rf8 3 Nh6 mate. If Rxf5 2 Qxh4. If
1...Qg5 2 Rd8+ Rf8 (Qxd8 3 Nh6+) 3 Rxf8+ Kxf8 4 Qc5+ is also decisive.

Bled Olympiad 2002.

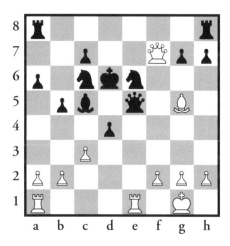

1 Be7+! and Black is mated after Nxe7 2 Rxe5 Kxe5 3 Re1+ Kd6 4 Qxe6 or 1…Kd5 2 Qf3+ Kc4 3 b3.

Vishy Anand vs. Ye Jiangchuan

Asian team championship, Kuala Lumpur 1989.

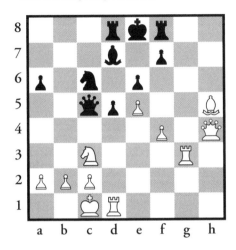

1 Bxf7+! If Kxf7 2 Qh5+ Ke7 3 Rg7 leads to mate, as does Rxf7 2 Rg8+ Rf8 3 Qh5+ Ke7 4 Rg7+ Rf7 5 Qxf7 mate.

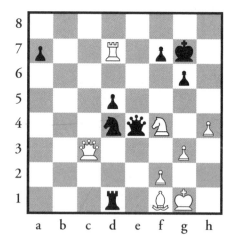

1 Rxd5? Rxf1+ 2 Kxf1 Qh1 mate.